The Treatment
of Prisoners and
Prison Conditions

Series Titles

- **The History of Punishment and Imprisonment**
- **Juveniles Growing Up in Prison**
- **Political Prisoners**
- **Prison Alternatives and Rehabilitation**
- **Prison Conditions Around the World**
- **The Treatment of Prisoners and Prison Conditions**
- **The True Cost of Prisons**
- **Unequal Justice**
- **Women Incarcerated**

The Treatment of Prisoners and Prison Conditions

BY **Roger Smith**

FOREWORD BY **Larry E. Sullivan, PhD**

Associate Dean, John Jay College of Criminal Justice

MASON CREST

Mason Crest
450 Parkway Drive, Suite D
Broomall, PA 19008
www.masoncrest.com

Printed and bound in the United States of America.

First printing
9 8 7 6 5 4 3 2 1

Series ISBN: 978-1-4222-3781-6
Hardcover ISBN: 978-1-4222-3787-8
ebook ISBN: 978-1-4222-8002-7

Cataloging-in-Publication Data is available on file at the Library of Congress.

Developed and Produced by Print Matters Productions, Inc.
(www.printmattersinc.com)

Cover and Interior Design: Tom Carling, Carling Design
Additional Text: Brian Boone

Contents

Foreword by Larry E. Sullivan, PhD 6

1 An Introduction to Prison 9

2 Overcrowding 21

3 Disease 33

4 Violence 47

5 Excessive Force 59

Series Glossary 75

Further Resources 78

Index 79

About the Author, Series Consultant, and Picture Credits.............. 80

KEY ICONS TO LOOK FOR:

Words to understand: These words with their easy-to-understand definitions will increase the reader's understanding of the text while building vocabulary skills.

Sidebars: This boxed material within the main text allows readers to build knowledge, gain insights, explore possibilities, and broaden their perspectives by weaving together additional information to provide realistic and holistic perspectives.

Educational Videos: Readers can view videos by scanning our QR codes, providing them with additional educational content to supplement the text. Examples include news coverage, moments in history, speeches, iconic sports moments and much more!

Text-dependent questions: These questions send the reader back to the text for more careful attention to the evidence presented there.

Research projects: Readers are pointed toward areas of further inquiry connected to each chapter. Suggestions are provided for projects that encourage deeper research and analysis.

Series glossary of key terms: This back-of-the-book glossary contains terminology used throughout this series. Words found here increase the reader's ability to read and comprehend higher-level books and articles in this field.

Foreword

Prisons have a long history, one that began with the idea of evil, guilt, and atonement. In fact, the motto of one of the first prison reform organizations was "Sin no more." Placing offenders in prison was, for most of the history of prison systems, a ritual for redemption through incarceration; hence the language of punishment takes on a very religious cast. The word *penitentiary* itself comes from the concept of penance, or self-punishment to make up for a past wrong. When we discuss prisons, we are dealing not only with the law, but with very strong emotions and reactions to acts that range from minor crimes, or misdemeanors, to major crimes, or felonies, such as murder and rape.

Prisons also reflect the level of the civilizing process through which a culture travels, and it tells us much about how we treat our fellow human beings. The 19th-century Russian author Fyodor Dostoyevsky, who was a political prisoner, remarked, "The degree of civilization in a society can be measured by observing its prisoners." Similarly, Winston Churchill, the British prime minister during World War II, said that the "treatment of crime and criminals is one of the most unfailing tests of civilization of any country."

For much of the history of the American prison, we tried to rehabilitate or modify the criminal behavior of offenders through a variety of treatment programs. In the last quarter of the 20th century, politicians and citizens alike realized that this attempt had failed, and they began passing stricter laws, imprisoning people for longer terms, and building more prisons. This movement has taken a great toll on society. Beginning in the 1970s federal and state governments passed mandatory minimum sentencing laws, stricter habitual offender legislation, and other "tough on crime" laws that have led today to the incarceration in prisons and jails of approximately 2.3 million people, or an imprisonment rate of 720 per 100,000 people, the highest recorded level in the world. This has led to the overcrowding of prisons, worse living conditions, fewer educational programs, and severe budgetary problems. Imprisonment carries a significant social cost since it splits families and contributes to a cycle of crime, violence, drug addiction, and poverty. The Federal Sentencing Reform Act of 1984 created a grid of offenses and crime categories for sentencing that disallowed mitigating circumstances. This grid was meant to prevent disparate sentences for similar crimes. The government made these guidelines mandatory, thereby taking most discretionary sentencing out of the hands of judges who previously could give a wider range of sentences, such as one year to life, and allow for some type of rehabilitation. The unintended consequences of this legislative reform in sentencing was the doubling of the number of incarcerated people in the United States. Combined with the harsh sentences on drug offenders, almost half of the prisoners in the federal system are narcotics offenders, both violent and nonviolent, traffickers and users. States followed suit in enacting the harsh guidelines of the federal government in sentencing patterns. "Life without parole" laws and the changes in parole and probation practices led to even more offenders behind bars. Following the increase in the number of incarcerated offenders, more and more prisons were built with the aid of federal funds and filled to the brim with both violent and nonviolent offenders. In addition, many states handed over penal custody to the new private for-profit prisons that stemmed from mass incarceration.

In the 21st century officials, politicians, and the public began to realize that such drastic laws wrought much harm to society. With the spread of long-term imprisonment, those who had spent decades in prison were unemployable after release. Their criminal histories followed them and made it difficult if not impossible to find gainful employment. Therefore, they entered the criminal world continually and thus sped up the vicious cycle of crime-imprisonment-release-crime-punishment. America was reaching the tipping point; something had to give.

In response to this growing trend of harsh sentencing, for example, the Supreme Court led the way between 2005 and 2016 with decisions banning the death penalty for juveniles (Roper v. Simmons, U.S. 551 [2005]), life sentence without parole for juveniles not convicted of homicide (Graham v. Florida, 130 S. Ct. 2011 [2010]); and life without parole for juveniles (Miller v. Alabama and Jackson v. Hobbes 132 S. Ct. 2455 [2012] and Montgomery v. Louisiana 135 S.Ct. 1729 [2015]). Behavioral psychologists and other officials do not consider juveniles capable of making fully formed decisions, and the Supreme Court has recognized the developmental differences that excuses full individual responsibility and applies to their actions the philosophic principle of just deserts. Many states (90 percent of prisoners are under state, not federal jurisdiction) are beginning to take action by reducing harsh mandatory sentences for adults. Most states, for example, have gone toward the decriminalization or legalization of marijuana, with lighter penalties for possession of the drug. Since most prisoners in state institutions are violent, however, contemporary America is caught in a dilemma with which many academics and governmental policy makers are aggressively grappling.

All these are reasons why this series on the prison system is extremely important for understanding the history and culture of the United States. Readers will learn all facets of punishment: its history; the attempts to rehabilitate offenders; the increasing number of women and juveniles in prison; the inequality of sentencing among the races; attempts to find alternatives to incarceration; the high cost, both economically and morally, of imprisonment; and other equally important issues. These books teach us the importance of understanding that the prison system affects more people in the United States than any institution, other than our schools.

LARRY E. SULLIVAN, PHD
Associate Dean
Chief Librarian
John Jay College of Criminal Justice
Professor of Criminal Justice
Graduate School and University Center
City University of New York

1 An Introduction to Prison

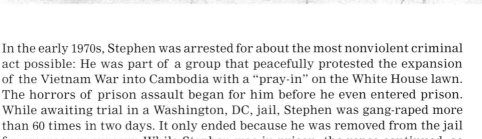

Words to Understand

Berated: Scolded someone vigorously and lengthily.

Disposition: Settlement of a legal matter.

Geriatric: Relating to senior citizens.

Sociopaths: People whose behavior is antisocial and who lack a conscience.

In the early 1970s, Stephen was arrested for about the most nonviolent criminal act possible: He was part of a group that peacefully protested the expansion of the Vietnam War into Cambodia with a "pray-in" on the White House lawn. The horrors of prison assault began for him before he even entered prison. While awaiting trial in a Washington, DC, jail, Stephen was gang-raped more than 60 times in two days. It only ended because he was removed from the jail for emergency surgery. While Stephen was in prison, the rapes continued, as prison staff looked the other way or, as Stephen alleges, purposely housed certain inmates together because they knew rape would be more likely. Stephen was raped in eight different prisons, which led him to contract HIV. He later died of an AIDS-related illness.

What Are Prisons?

Prisons vary in security from double-barred steel cages inside high-walled, high-security fortresses to unlocked rooms in buildings surrounded by open fields. Prisoners' experiences of discomfort vary from living in sensory-deprived isolation in windowless, tiny rooms to living at work camps with no physical adversity. There are prisons that are like farms where prisoners spend their days working, unwatched, in the community. There are "weekend prisons" and "day prisons," and there are prisons with tediously boring routines broken only by incidents of violence and cruelty. There are prisons where the only exercise allowed is an hour

A guard locks down a hallway in a Serbian prison.

of walking in an outdoor cage several times a week, and then there are prisons with tennis courts. There are prisons that are remarkably crowded and prisons of isolation. The most common prisons are overcrowded ones near large cities where the boring routines are interspersed with outbreaks of abuse and violence.

The prisoner tried to look tough as he walked to 7 Block, but he did not look tough enough. Some older men pretending to be friendly invited him that first night to have some homemade liquor. They spiked it with Thorazine, and the boy became the evening's entertainment: the men gang-raped him. From that night on, one of the prisoners forced him to be his boy. He could not tell the guards because inmates kill snitches in prison. The complacent guards and administrators saw things and did nothing about them. The prisoner, who is now a free man, told Just Detention International (JDI):

> I wish you could see how I've paid for that stupid opening line and fifty-three dollars over a quarter of a century ago. I wish I could allow you inside my experience for just a few minutes to see, and feel and fully understand the hell that lives with me every day . . . my shame, low self- esteem, self-hatred, deep-seated rage, and inability to trust have gone unabated for years.

According to JDI, inmates rape approximately 1 in 10 males. JDI attributes this in part to the overcrowding and understaffing in many prisons.

Prison by the Numbers

Writers often use the terms *jail* and *prison* interchangeably when describing places of incarceration. Prisons are generally federal or state institutions that house convicted criminals serving long sentences, whereas cities or counties usually run jails. Authorities place people in jails who are awaiting a trial or a legal **disposition** or are serving a short sentence.

Different surveys report different numbers of people incarcerated, but all agree there are now more than two million U.S. citizens who are prisoners. According to Bill Moyers's 1970 PBS report, "Prisons in America," there were 338,029 inmates in the United States, but by 2010 the amount had soared to 2.3 million. The United States takes the lead for incarceration internationally with approximately 724 prisoners per 100,000 people; Russia follows in frequency of incarceration with 581 prisoners. Rounding out the top 5 are Ukraine (350), South Africa (334), and Poland (250). Both the United States and Canada have most Western and European countries beat, where the incarceration rates per 100,000 are lower: Australia (96), Germany (78), Switzerland (84), and the Netherlands (75).

Packed Prisons

Why the huge increase in the number of prisoners during the last few decades in the United States? According to Marc Mauer in *Americans Behind Bars: U.S. and International Use of Incarceration*, one cause might be a high rate of violent crime for which the country believes offenders should be imprisoned. Another cause could be stiffer punishments than those given for similar crimes in other nations.

Mississippi State Penitentiary, an American prison farm in Sunflower County, MS.

Jailer at the Old Melbourne Gaol, the Australian state of Victoria's oldest surviving penal establishment, which attracts approximately 140,000 visitors per year.

Norval Morris, in *The Oxford History of the Prison*, suggests that the rise in U.S. imprisonment is largely because of sentencing reforms. Because of a rise in crime during the late 1960s and early 1970s, a mentality of "get tough on crime" caused more criminals to be sentenced to prison for longer terms, and stiffer policies for drug arrests came into being. According to the FBI, almost 50 percent of federal prisoners are in prison for drug-related offenses. "Three strikes and you're out" laws for repeat offenders and "truth in sentencing" laws restricting early release also raised the prison population. Where once a parole board could release a prisoner at an earlier date than his maximum sentence, this became less likely in the 1980s. The public accused judges and parole boards of being too soft on criminals; consequently, parole officers began cracking down on parolees—oftentimes returning them to prison at the first sign of a parole offense. Through the 1980s and 1990s, the public experienced a growing fear of crime. Politicians noticed they could boost their popularity by opposing crime because no powerful group of voters is usually against a "get tough on crime agenda."

Crime Is Falling

According to a 2015 report from the Brookings Institution, the national crime rate peaked in 1991. Since that time, violent crime (murder, assault) has dropped by 51 percent, its lowest point in 45 years. Put another way, 79.8 people per every 1,000 were victims of violent crimes annually in the early 1990s. Today, that number sits at about 23 victimizations per 1,000.

Who's Who in Prison?

The two main groups involved in prison life are the prisoners and the staff. Each sees the other with some prejudice. Inmates view guards as stupid and authoritarian, and correctional officers see prisoners as corrupt, untrustworthy, and vicious.

The average age of inmates in the United States is 40. In the federal prisons, 93 percent are male. Thirty-five percent are Hispanic, 34 percent are black, 27 percent are white, and the rest are Native American, Asian, or "other." The Federal Bureau of Prisons (FBOP) lists 70 percent of U.S. inmates as American; 20 percent as Colombian, Mexican, or Cuban; and 10 percent as coming from other countries.

Aging prisoners are a growing population. In the state of Arizona more than 5,000 graying inmates are behind bars, and the state must pay for all their medical needs. Arizona is a mirror of a national problem: states are trying to find ways to pay for the mounting medical costs of aging prison populations. Approximately 16 states have special housing units for **geriatric** inmates.

An inmate is separated from the world by a chain link fence and concertina wire.

Prisoners find out quickly that the main dividing line in the institution is race. Black prisoners stay with blacks, whites stay with whites, and Hispanics stay with Hispanics. If one strays into the other's turf, especially in facilities with very violent criminals, he may be beaten, raped, or killed.

America's Elderly Prisoner Boom

A California program enlists younger inmates to care for elderly ones.

Prison Terms

While slang varies from prison to prison, here is some common jargon used among inmates in American penitentiaries:

Ace boon coon: A prisoner's best buddy.

All day: A life sentence.

Fresh fish: New prisoners.

Badge: A prison guard.

Bug: An insane person who annoys other prisoners.

Catnap: A short prison term.

Snitch: A prisoner who tells the guards information on other prisoners.

Several subcultures can be found in prison. One group is international drug smugglers who do not see themselves as "criminals." Among this group are Cubans, Mexicans, Colombians, and Jamaicans. Another subgroup is made up of members of organized crime, which includes the Mafia. A third group is the bikers, which may include Hell's Angels, Pagans, Outlaws, Diablos, Satan's Slaves, and other motorcycle clubs. Thousands of these bikers are imprisoned.

Prison guards stand outside of the Dade County Men's Correctional Facility.

Correctional Officers' Difficult Job

A correctional officer's job is not easy. Authors Ross and Richards, in their book *Behind Bars: Surviving Prison*, describe a typical cellblock: "In every cellblock (typically 500 prisoners) there are a couple dozen seething paranoids and violent **sociopaths** who've armed themselves with deadly weapons." Gangs in prison keep guards on the constant lookout for violent outbreaks. Gang members coerce guards to smuggle drugs into prison for them: they have a friend on the outside take a picture of the guard's family and home, then show the photo and threaten violence to his family if he doesn't smuggle drugs to the gang.

Correctional officers often work long hours and are poorly paid. The job is one of the less desirable in law enforcement, and the best way for a guard to make a respectable income is to put in long hours of overtime. Many guards are stressed out, burned out, and cynical; most of them just want to get through their day with no problems. Usually, the only time the public notices correctional officers is when there is a prison riot or an escape.

A Misunderstood Profession

One writer, Ted Conover, who made it his mission to get inside the experience of a correctional officer, believes there are good guards and bad guards, and that the profession is misunderstood and underappreciated. Conover did not want to excuse abuse, but to help the public understand it in the context of a brutal system, he became a correctional officer at Sing Sing prison. He didn't tell his superiors or other guards about his project; they had no idea that he would be writing about his experience.

While Conover worked at Sing Sing, the job transformed him. Every morning when he woke up, he wondered if he would be hurt that day. He couldn't do the job and not jump in if a friend was in trouble. He began wanting to use brute strength against prisoners after seeing them attack other guards and disobey orders. He found prison to be full of frustration with very little outlet for the stress; the more he did the job, the more he wanted to use force: it felt like a release, a cleansing. He was torn between his duties as a correctional officer and as a person.

He tells of following a prisoner overburdened with laundry bags, wanting to help him—but officers are not allowed to help prisoners. A civilian passing by criticized him, and so feeling guilty, he helped the prisoner—but then the other guards **berated** him. In the end, he felt like he was neither a good guard nor a good person.

Conover found that correctional officers had many marital problems, and divorce was common among them. He thought that he could keep from having these difficulties, but he found that he became distant from his wife, becoming moody and silent. He tried to keep the horrors from her and his family, so he separated himself from them. When he came home having done things that made him feel dirty, he would act differently around his family and friends. It was a stigmatized job that involved actions so shameful that they were hidden out of sight.

Eventually, Ted Conover wrote a book called *Life as a Jailor*, describing his experience. Even after leaving his life as a guard, however, he has nightmares about the prison several times a week.

According to Jeffrey Ian Ross, who worked for more than 3 years in a correctional facility, and Stephen C. Richards, who spent 11 years in federal custody, the authors of *Behind Bars: Surviving Prison*, some guards are honorable and decent people, while others are not. A number of them come to work every day and treat prisoners with courtesy and respect. Some have earned the nicknames of "hacks" and "cops." A hack is an officer who does as little as possible, collects his paycheck, and goes home. A cop is a guard who is constantly trying to catch prisoners breaking petty rules. They will send prisoners to the hole (solitary confinement) "and another officer, a man who deserves your thanks, will get you out." The best guards are women and men who are level headed and treat prisoners with care. A few correctional officers have risked their jobs and the anger of other guards and administrators to stand up for the rights of inmates.

Victims of Prisoners

"I hope that someone will realize that the victims are the *true* prisoners . . . *not* the criminals. . . . I only wish the rapist would understand that I am in prison for the rest of my life. There is no parole. There is no time off for good behavior."

A woman wrote these words after she was raped and almost murdered. Her date was walking her to her apartment one night, when a man put a knife to his throat and forced the two into her apartment. She endured the next five hours of torture with a hunting knife and extreme sexual torture by a heroin addict.

She never got over it, although she has spent thousands and thousands of dollars on therapies, trying to ease her emotional trauma. She has seen the best doctors, taken medication, and joined 12-step groups. She is a religious person and forgives the man who did this, but nothing numbs the pain; she has never been able to get over it. She says she is permanently damaged, and that will never change.

Guard tower at Sing Sing Correctional Facility in Ossining, NY.

A father from Florida wrote on a prisoner advocacy website about a family friend who began molesting the father's two small sons when they were four and five years old. The molestation went on for two years until the man was found out, stopped, and sentenced to 11 consecutive life sentences. The police found in his possession a self-written manuscript on how to seduce, molest, and kill a child and make it look like an accident. Fortunately, the Florida boys were found before they were killed. The father writes in anger because the website expresses sympathy for both victims and criminals in prison. He says, "Do you feel sorrow for this man who will spend the rest of his life in prison? Do you really care if atrocities against him by other inmates may happen? Will you feel sorrow if he were murdered in that prison? I answer no to all of the above. . . . Now we have our life sentences to try and straighten out our boys' lives."

Tragedies such as these have occurred in the lives of many in North America. Our prisons have countless inmates living out the rest of their years in prison for destroying the lives of other people. Some members of the general public feel prisoners deserve to suffer the rest of their lives and that poor prison conditions are what they deserve.

Rehabilitation versus Punishment

Inmates from Dade County Men's Correctional Facility spend time outside under the close eye of a correctional officer.

The authors of *Behind Bars: Surviving Prison* believe that many prison administrators in the United States have given up on rehabilitation; instead, "they devote their budgets to cement, bricks, and steel to build more facilities to house a growing prisoner population." These authors believe that most wardens seem to have limited their efforts to the safety and custody problems of their prisons. Thankfully, they say, some prison staff come to work each day and try to help individual prisoners, through conversation, operating specific programs, or setting a good example. They find fulfillment in assisting inmates to grow and learn the skills and attitudes needed to live useful, law-abiding lives.

Some citizens think that efforts to rehabilitate prisoners, such as college courses, parenting classes, vocational training, and psychological therapy, are undeserved privileges for lawbreakers, whereas others see rehabilitation as a way to reform convicts and reduce crime. The treatment of inmates ultimately affects the rest of society. Prisons in the United States release 650,000 prisoners every year. If overcrowding, disease, violence, and abuse are rampant in prisons, and if these conditions irreparably harm the men and women who eventually return to society, then society suffers.

Text-Dependent Questions

1. Of all the different types of prison, which are the most common?
2. What's the major difference between a prison and a jail?
3. What's the main political reason for why prisons started becoming overcrowded in the 1980s?

Research Projects

1. Find more prisoner slang. Research the terms' meanings and origins.
2. Are "rich people prisons" real? What are some features found there that are not found in other prisons?

Overcrowding

One day the world of Victor Hassine, author of *Life Without Parole: Living in Prison Today*, suddenly turned upside down. Without warning, his cell door opened and prison guards sent another man inside. Victor had been in Pennsylvania's prison system for over 12 years and was doing well, as he put it, in his routine of "working, obeying, and vegetating." He had been in a single cell until that day.

The first argument the cellmates had was over who got the top or bottom bunk. Next, they fought over when they would turn the lights on or off, toilet hygiene habits, property storage, cell cleaning, and when friends could visit. Every day they argued over missing property. Their waking hours were filled with accusations of stealing, snoring, bodily noises, or smoking—and every day they found something more to argue about.

Hassine's experiences were not unique. As prisons became more crowded, authorities placed prisoners together based merely on their race or age or cell availability. Inmates did not have the chance to interview potential cellmates. Living so closely together, personal differences were bound to grate on prisoners' nerves.

What Is Overcrowding?

Victor Hassine says *prison overcrowding* is an overused term describing a collection of conditions that disrupt prisons all over the United States. He says such words do not make the reality clear to the public. The public usually sees it as a vague *social problem*, a softened term that does not define the "extreme, hopeless, horrifying, and tragic conditions that truly exist. The blood and guts of what prison overcrowding is inside and what it really does to the insiders remains an **enigma** to most outsiders."

A prison cell block at New Mexico State Penitentiary.

Jimmy Lerner, author of the book *You Got Nothing Coming*, describes his cell in a Nevada state prison: it was 8 by 6 feet with a 12-foot ceiling, a fluorescent light bulb with a mesh screen around it, and a stainless-steel toilet (with no cover) connected to a sink unit. The cinder block walls in his cell were yellow-brown from years of cigarette smoke, and there was much "moronic graffiti." He says, "I've always had a mild case of claustrophobia, but until cell 47 in the Fish Tank [in prison jargon, fish are prisoners, and the prison is the fish tank] it had never been more than a minor inconvenience. With the beds jutting out 3 feet from the wall, only one man at a time could comfortably stand up." He had heard of the chronic problem of prison overcrowding before, but the issue seemed as far removed from his life as the atrocities reported in the Balkans. He goes on to say, "The issue had a bit more immediacy now."

In many correctional facilities, prisoners are double bunked in cells meant for one person. In some prisons, inmates sleep in cold prison gyms or on the floors of basements, halls, and dayrooms. Some prisons use tents or sleep prisoners in the same bunks at different times of the day.

Overcrowding is a concern in Canadian prisons as well. The Canadian Church Council on Justice and Corrections website tells of an incident in a Toronto jail where authorities housed three men convicted of a violent armed robbery in pretrial custody for approximately 10 months in a 6- by 9-foot jail cell meant for single occupancy. Authorities allowed for a shorter sentence because of the difficult, overcrowded conditions. Not only were the cells too small for three men, but the guards allowed the men to go outside for recreation only once a week. The rules stipulate that authorities should let prisoners out for 20 minutes a day, but due to understaffing, this was impossible.

The Numbers behind Overcrowding

According to *Prisons and Jails: A Deterrent to Crime?*, U.S. federal prisons were at 31 percent over capacity in 2000. By 2013, that number had grown to 40 percent. Overcrowding is also an issue in juvenile residential facilities. More than a third of juvenile detention centers had more residents than available beds. Most states reported having some overcrowding in their facilities. Mississippi had the least overcrowding, with facilities at 50 percent capacity, and Alabama had the most at 192 percent capacity.

Reasons for Overcrowding

Between 1970 and 1994, U.S. state and federal lawmakers made a big change in sentencing practices. In the 1960s, laws set the maximum time a person could serve in prison for different offenses. A judge could sentence a person to less than this amount but not more, and a parole board later decided the actual time a prisoner would serve. The parole board made its decision when to release the prisoner based on the severity of the person's crime, how well the prisoner behaved in prison, and how well the board thought the person would do in society. Released prisoners would then have a certain amount of time to be on parole after getting out of prison. Prison terms were not set in concrete because the basic belief was that incarceration would reform the prisoner. If a prisoner accepted help in prison from the available educational, vocational, and psychological training, authorities might release him at an earlier date.

During the late 1960s and early 1970s, however, attitudes changed. A series of articles published in the United States claimed that prisoners were unable to be reformed; the idea that a criminal could not change became popular. At the same time, crime increased, and lawmakers and politicians began to believe greater punishments could stop this trend. The press portrayed judges and parole boards as being too easy on criminals. Reformers recommended that governments eliminate parole boards and make prisoners serve mandatory sentences. Legislatures and judges agreed on "truth in sentencing." This meant that inmates would have to serve their full sentence, rather than serving only a small fraction of their term, being released on parole after sentencing, or having their sentence commuted to probation and serving none of their time. Then, in the 1980s, authorities cut rehabilitation programs in prisons and social services for parolees. Although crime rates in the 2000s and 2010s were significantly lower than in the 1980s and 1990s, the rates of imprisonment increased because of these sentencing reforms.

Police Discrimination

Evidence indicates that racial minorities still suffer discrimination at the hands of the police. Officers are more likely to shoot, kill, arrest, or physically abuse people of color. In 2015, American police officers killed more than 100 unarmed African American citizens, compared to about 20 unarmed white citizens. Officers who are guilty of these behaviors often do not receive punishment for their misdeeds, as was the case with the high-profile police shooting deaths of Michael Brown, Freddie Gray, and Tamir Rice, among others.

Parole boards are still in place in the prison system. If an inmate has served his or her minimum sentence, a parole board reviews the case to decide if the inmate is ready for society. If the board thinks a release is acceptable, it comes up with a release plan. This plan will often specify that the person remain free of drugs and alcohol, stay away from other ex-offenders, and remain employed. Parolees must report regularly to a parole officer; those who violate terms or commit any new crime will be returned to prison.

According to Kelly Virella, one of the authors of *Prison Nation: The Warehousing of America's Poor*, parole officers have a stake in catching parolees who violate the conditions of their release. To keep their job, they have to catch offenders and put them back in prison. Some officers show lenience and fairness, but many officers reincarcerate at the first sign that an ex-prisoner has violated any parole conditions. Over 50 percent of men released from prison return within the first year and 70 percent within three years. Many parolees are returned to prison for technical violations of parole rules, such as failure to report to their officer, being unemployed, testing positive for illegal drugs, or not paying court costs.

Racial Overcrowding

By 2010 73 percent of U.S. prison and jail inmates were ethnic or racial minorities. About 12 percent of all black men age 25 to 29 were in jails or prisons. For Hispanics, it was 3 percent, and for white men in that age group it was under 2 percent.

Blacks are arrested at an unusually high rate compared to whites for violent crimes, such as murder, rape, and robbery. The criminal justice process treats minorities more severely than white offenders; an example of this is the greater likelihood that minorities will receive the death penalty. In some regions of the country, police departments tolerate excessive force directed at racial minorities. Authorities tend to treat members of racial minorities who are young, male, unemployed, and convicted of violent crimes or drug offenses more harshly than whites who commit these crimes or have these characteristics.

Research shows that times have changed. Before the 1960s, **blatant** discrimination ruled. The authors of *The Color of Justice: Race, Ethnicity and Crime in America*, Samuel Walker, Cassia Spohn, and Miriam DeLone do not believe that society has erased racial bigotry from the justice system, but it has diminished. In the 21st century, if a white man commits a crime against a black man, he is not above the law, and if a black man commits a crime against a white man, he will not receive justice at the hand of a white **lynch mob**.

Research shows that discrimination exists in the court system as well. Some judges give harsher sentences to black offenders who murder or rape whites and more lenient sentences if the crime was against a fellow black. In some cases, people of color are more likely to get prison, whereas whites may get only probation. In part because of these discriminatory sentencing practices, a much larger number of blacks are incarcerated in U.S. jails and prisons.

Effects of Overcrowding

Overcrowding affects all the other issues of prison life—disease, violence, and abuse. Willie Wilson, an author included in *Prison Nation: The Warehousing of America's Poor*, writes that most prison inmates have histories of drug and alcohol use and have been victims of sexual, emotional, and physical abuse. They do not come to prison with "highly developed coping mechanisms" and cannot get away from the stress around them to be alone and reflect or think. Many of them are mentally ill; in California alone, there are more than 32,000 mentally ill prisoners. When all these prisoners are overcrowded, the effects can be devastating. Kara Gotsch, public policy coordinator of the National Prison Project, says, "Overcrowding is one component that contributes to many different problems."

Due to overcrowding in an Oregon prison, authorities moved 78 women to an Arizona detention center. The new prison was mostly a men's facility and lacked a separate unit for women. Instead, the prison used a medical quarantine room close to the hospital area for this purpose. According to 5 women in this group, guards sexually abused women for months, and no one stopped the abuse. The situation started when a guard captain gave 6 women marijuana joints. He returned with several other guards and told the women that these officers would search their cells. To avoid charges of possession for marijuana, the correctional officers forced the women to perform a strip tease. In the end, 50 guards were involved in the incident—from starting the abuse to covering it up. They transported 5 of the women back to Oregon in an attempt to keep the matter quiet, but one of the women told her story to *Prison Legal News*. Five women eventually filed a suit in Tucson against the prison and 15 employees. According to the book *Prison Nation*, degradation of this sort is common in prisons.

When officials confine too many prisoners to a space, sanitation also declines, and inmates become more susceptible to disease. Prison experts also believe that overcrowding is distressing to inmates, which leads to violence. Kara Gotsch says, "Prisons are very violent, unsafe and damaging places. A person goes in and is never the same."

Because of crowding, Pleasant Valley State Prison houses level-three prisoners (inmates with longer sentences, prior prison terms, or special behavior problems) in a gymnasium where they sleep in triple bunk beds with little space between each bed. In 2003, news broke of a riot involving 300 inmates in one of its recreation yards. The situation got so out of hand that a guard resorted to deadly force, shooting and killing a 28-year-old prisoner who was serving 15 years to life for second-degree murder. Staff justified the shooting on the grounds that the inmate was threatening the lives of other inmates and was armed. However, security camera footage and eyewitness accounts place the riot's head count at about 50, and show that no one, not even the man who was shot, had weapons.

Solutions

Both the United States and Canada agree that one of the main ways to stop prison overcrowding is to send fewer people to prison. The Canadian Criminal Justice Association (CCJA) has called on all criminal justice authorities and the public to consider how to decrease overcrowding. A number of jurisdictions are already working to make changes. CCJA is encouraging the communities to try more tactics of crime prevention. They are advocating that authorities use imprisonment as one of several options—not the only option. CCJA hopes that authorities will work more to help inmates successfully reintegrate into society. This may decrease the return rate of prisoners.

Swap-out Programs

A look at how swap-out programs could ease prison overcrowding.

Inmates in an Orleans Parish Prison yard in New Orleans, LA.

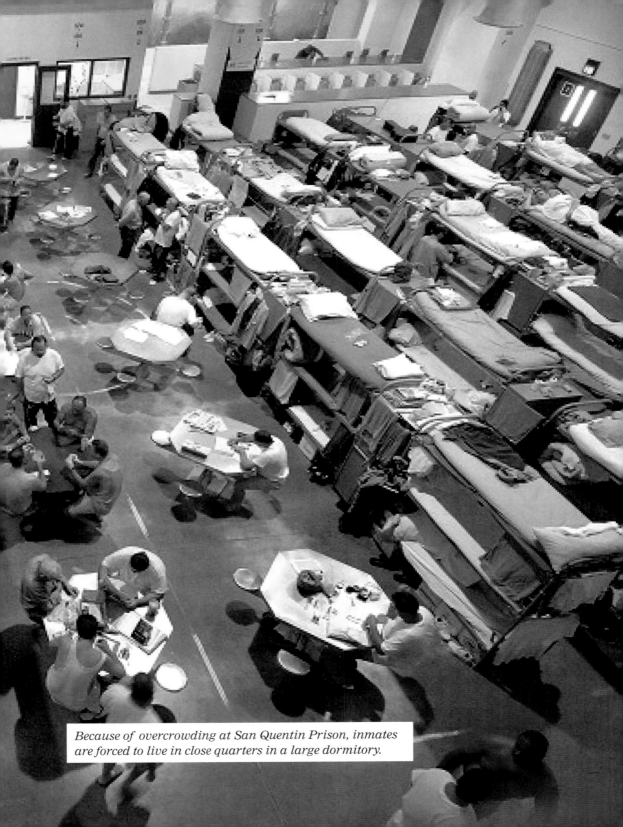

Because of overcrowding at San Quentin Prison, inmates are forced to live in close quarters in a large dormitory.

The Convict Code

The following is a list of dos and don'ts that prisoners should follow if they want to survive among other inmates.

DON'T:
- Break your promises.
- Snitch on other prisoners.
- Lose your head.
- Take advantage of fellow convicts.
- Pressure other prisoners.

DO:
- Be loyal to prisoners as a group.
- Be honorable.
- Pay any debts.
- Be a man.
- Mind your own business.
- Play it cool.
- Do your own time.
- Watch your words.
- Be aware at all times.
- Be tough.

The group Human Rights Watch in the United States also believes solutions can be found to prison overcrowding. This group wants states to reexamine their sentencing policies: shorter sentences for prisoners might be wise, fair, and more cost-effective. Human Rights Watch encourages the total elimination of mandatory minimum sentences and asks courts to consider alternatives to imprisonment. The group's view is that incarceration is often unnecessary and damages many inmates. Group members are working to persuade officials to consider their recommendations and make the necessary changes.

Alternative forms of sentencing are now widely used in many states. Instead of prison, authorities are offering some first-time offenders a choice of alternative sentences. Some of these include boot camp, community service programs, fines, day reporting centers, work release, **weekend sentencing**, electronic monitoring, house arrest, and residential community corrections.

Canada has used alternative sentencing for years; it refers to this practice as "sentencing options." The most common option is a fine: authorities fine 45 percent of the adult offenders eligible for sentencing alternatives. Probation, restitution, community service, conditional sentence (community service), and intermittent imprisonment, such as weekend prison, are some of the other alternative sentences used to help keep prison crowding down.

Unfortunately, overcrowding continues to be an all-too-real issue for North American prisoners. It contributes to many other problems, including the spread of diseases between prisoners. In a population prone to mental illnesses, over-crowding intensifies these problems as well.

Text-Dependent Questions

1. What are some of the places prisoners sleep because there aren't enough beds in cells?
2. What state has the biggest problem with overcrowding?
3. What percentage of male parolees return to prison within a year? Three years?

Research Projects

1. Find more examples of dos and don'ts in "the convict code."
2. Find a few more examples of firsthand accounts of prison overcrowding. What are some of the subject's unique problems with serving time in an overcrowded prison?

3 Disease

At Lancaster Prison in California, a prisoner walks his dog every day, tugging at the leash in a zigzag pattern across the prison yard. His bloodshot eyes glance wildly as he talks continuously to his little dog. The other men sneer and make fun of him as he shuffles by. They don't pet the dog because it is not really there.

Before starting his day, the dog-owner gets out of bed, beats his chest to kill the wicked pig living in there, and stuffs all his important papers in his waistband. He goes for weeks without a shower. When he leaves the cafeteria, he spins around and knocks three times on the table before leaving. He has conversations with people only he can see, often cursing and spitting. He is one of thousands of mentally ill prisoners in California state prisons.

Prisoners with mental illnesses are often inadequately treated or not treated at all due to shortages in qualified staff members and specialized facilities. Prisoners with more traditional illnesses fare little better. For example, at California's Pleasant Valley State Prison when an inmate became ill, his condition was not even correctly diagnosed for several weeks. His wife confided to the *Fresno Bee* newspaper how guards pushed him along with other prisoners through the medical care facility "like cattle" and then the doctor told him it was just a cold. Later, other doctors told him it was pneumonia, but eventually, doctors determined he was suffering from Valley fever, an illness spread by a fungus. Despite what is shown in these examples, all prisoners have the constitutional right to receive proper medical care, whether psychiatric care or general health care.

Approximately one in every six prisoners in the United States is mentally ill, and many suffer from serious disorders, such as schizophrenia, depression, or bipolar disorder.

In many cases, prison medical workers have lost their rights to practice medicine in outside society. Some doctors have had their medical licenses revoked or have been convicted of a crime in another state. In an overcrowded system, the staff often believes that prisoners' medical requests are attention-seeking behaviors or a way to get drugs; therefore, staff ignores some medical requests. Prisons have an overall pattern of poor health care, and this neglect affects the lives of prisoners and may eventually affect society in general when authorities release these inmates.

Mental Illness in America's Prisons

Inmates with mental illness tell their stories.

Mentally Ill Prisoners

Approximately one in every six prisoners in the United States is mentally ill, and many suffer from serious illnesses, such as **schizophrenia**, depression, or **bipolar disorder**. Human Rights Watch found that most mentally ill prisoners are not adequately treated or are not treated at all. Some mentally ill prisoners who are undertreated or untreated suffer painful symptoms: they curl up silently in their cells; they babble, rant, and rave; or they hallucinate and live in invisible worlds. They cover themselves in feces, pound their head against walls, and self-mutilate their body. Some of them commit suicide. In many prisons, the facilities are not specialized for mental illness, and there is a shortage of staff.

Why Prisons Are Filled with Mentally Ill Inmates

How did so many people with mental illness end up in prison? In the United States, it started in the 1960s with a process called "deinstitutionalization," when mental health institutions released many of their patients. The originators of this idea imagined that community-based mental health services would be in place to help these released patients, but the services were never set up. In the end, deinstitutionalization meant that a flood of homeless people with mental illness or addictions roamed city streets, unable to find help. When they went untreated, their emotional stability went downhill quickly, and many ended up breaking the law.

Once people with mental illness become criminal offenders in the United States, they face a system that sends people to prison even for low-level, nonviolent crimes. Human Rights Watch believes U.S. prisons are not set up for the special needs of the mentally ill, so these patients are often victims of violence and **extortion** by other inmates or guards. When a prisoner with mental illness breaks the rules too many times, guards put him in solitary confinement where he spends up to 24 hours in a small, sometimes windowless, cell. Long periods of solitary confinement are hard to endure for people who are healthy, but such treatment can cause mentally ill prisoners to break down completely. When that happens, authorities take them to psychiatric hospitals for treatment, but they often return to solitary confinement—and the cycle begins all over again.

Canadian Association of Elizabeth Fry Societies (CAEFS) has a mission to help criminalized women and girls in the justice system. Kim Pate, CAEFS' executive director and a teacher and lawyer, shares her experience in a Web article called "Prisons as Panacea." As a student, she volunteered to tutor female prisoners and psychiatric patients. When she started out, she had no idea how many days and nights for the next 20 years she would spend kneeling in front of metal doors and meal slots trying to help prisoners. She found some prisoners slashing their body, shackled, or banging their head against the wall. "Nor could I have imagined the utter disdain with which others, be they correctional authorities, members of parliament, or academics might regard calls for the law to be upheld in the treatment of prisoners."

Pate cites the downsizing of mental health facilities as a major reason for the incarceration of a growing number of women with psychological disabilities. She says that when officials put these women out on the streets, their efforts to survive, self-medicate, and cope often lead them down the wrong avenues and into prisons.

Help Is on the Way

An important milestone in prison mental health in the United States occurred on October 30, 2004, when President George W. Bush signed the Mentally Ill Offender Treatment and Crime Reduction Act. The act gave $50 million in grant money to help make sure juvenile and adult nonviolent offenders with mental illness receive correct diagnoses and receive the treatment they need from the time of their arrest until their release into the community. The grant has helped to establish more mental health courts and give more funds for pretrial jail diversion programs. Resources have also gone to improve the overall quality of mental health care in prisons and jails. In 2013, the Act was reauthorized to provide an additional $40 million in federal funding through 2019.

The Canadian National Committee for Police/Mental Health Liaison (CNCP-MHL) is an organization of police officers and mental health professionals providing information, services, and support to police officers. Since police officers are the first officials who make contact with offenders who have a mental illness, they can benefit from special training. The main goal of the CNCPMHL is to help guard against the unnecessary "criminalization" of the mentally ill. The committee teaches police how to direct offenders to the system that is best for them in their circumstances. For example, if a crime has been committed, police might direct an offender to the criminal justice system—but if the person was clearly not a danger to society, she might instead be sent to the mental health system for treatment. In some cases, offenders might be released if they are not dangerous and they so choose.

Prisoners with HIV/AIDS

In case after case I reviewed, prisoners were deliberately denied the standard medical treatment for HIV infection. It is my professional opinion that the grossly inappropriate care currently being provided is resulting in unnecessary pain and suffering and will be responsible for unnecessary deaths for patients who would respond to appropriate treatment.

All those known to have AIDS at the Limestone Correctional Facility are confined to a converted old warehouse with high, leaky ceilings, and double bunks so close together that they foster infection. They are constantly segregated and excluded from programs that other inmates participate in.

This is the testimony of Dr. Robert Cohen for the plaintiffs in a case concerning the Mississippi State Prison (MSP) Parchman Farm. Dr. Cohen has been the director of the Montefiore Rikers Island Health Service in New York State, overseeing the care of 15,000 inmates. He has also reviewed medical care for the Department of Justice.

In 1999, Parchman became involved in a lawsuit filed by HIV-positive patients. Patients claimed that the medical care they were receiving was threatening their lives. The issue revolved mainly around the drugs prescribed at the prison. Since 1996, the basic government recommendation for AIDS and HIV medications urged a three-drug combination therapy; using one or two drugs was greatly discouraged. Some state incarceration facilities, however, such as MSP Parchman, do not allow three-drug treatments. At Parchman, the rules required prisoners to take two-drug therapy for six months before officials allowed the third drug (called a protease inhibitor). Even prisoners who had been on three drugs successfully before coming to prison had to go back on two. Dr. Cohen reported that adding a third drug to two failing drugs is usually proven to start an early development of resistance to HIV drugs. "This is almost always the wrong approach, and it is the only approach taken at MSP Parchman," wrote Dr. Cohen. Unfortunately, the policies at Parchman are common in U.S. prisons. The lawsuit resulted in a court injunction that led to more intensive health care for HIV-positive inmates at Parchman, as well as ending the prison's practice of keeping HIV-positive prisoners segregated from the general population.

An inmate in the Florida prison system came to prison HIV positive, and officials gave him his medications. However, he received them at mealtime. The prisoner had carefully researched medications before serving his time, and he knew he had to wait an hour after taking the pills to eat because they were 77 percent less effective if he took them with food. Given prison procedures, he had the choice of skipping his breakfast to save his health or making his illness worse. The medications also came at the wrong time at night, so he kept the pills in his mouth and then put them into his pocket to take later. This was risky behavior; authorities could have locked him up in disciplinary confinement for trying to stay alive—yet taking the medications in the wrong way could have killed him. The American Civil Liberties Union helped find a solution to the problem. After serving his time in the prison system, his comment was, "The judge gave me 10 years, he didn't sentence me to death."

It's the official policy of the Federal Bureau of Prisons that all imprisoned people be offered HIV testing. However, as of 2016 only 5 of Louisiana's 104 parish (county) jails provide the service to inmates. Officials say that while testing is within budgetary constraints, treating the high number of potential HIV-positive inmates would be something the jails couldn't afford. So they'd rather just not test and not know. This is an especially troubling policy for Louisiana, which has one of the highest rates of HIV infections in the United States as well as one of the highest rates of incarceration.

Providing Proper HIV/AIDS Care

The Centers for Disease Control and Prevention estimates the AIDS rate in U.S. prisons is five times higher than in the general population. In a report, the National Commission on AIDS stated that by choosing mass imprisonment as the federal and state response for drug offenders, the prison system is getting more and more inmates with HIV. In 2014, 50 percent of incarcerations were for drug offenses. According to the website AIDSInfo.net, 17 percent of people living with AIDS in the United Sates have been in jails or prisons.

The United States Medical Center for federal prisoners in Springfield, MO.

The HIV/AIDS Legal Network in Canada says that, overall, most Canadian prisons provide good care for patients with HIV/AIDS and many times send them to outside sources for care. However, some patients say the care they receive is below public standards. Some Canadian prisons are not well equipped to deal with inmates who need long-term care, nor can they handle the increasing number of patients who are ill. Prisons also have difficulty getting experimental drugs and alternative therapies.

What's more, prison exposes inmates to AIDS in a variety of ways. Illicit drugs are common in prisons, and syringes are difficult to come by so often they are shared, infecting many people. Unprotected sex is another risk factor in contracting AIDS—and according to the Bureau of Justice Statistics, up to 40 percent are victims of sexual attacks. Such figures might be higher, since not all prisoners report sexual abuse to officials.

Each year approximately 650,000 U.S. prisoners finish their sentences and return to society. Inmates with AIDS may return to risk-taking behaviors if they are not educated and do not have good support. This can be a hazard to society and to themselves, as they may decline in health or return to prison. When authorities deny prisoners their medications or cause them to miss treatments, serious consequences to the general population can occur. Cynthia Chandler, founder of the Positive Women's Network (formerly the Women's Positive Legal Action Network) in Oakland, CA, says, "It would not surprise me if we start finding large amounts of drug-resistant HIV because of people coming back into their communities after having been denied their medications while in prison."

The "Silent Epidemic"—Hepatitis C

Hepatitis C (HCV) is now the most common bloodborne disease in the United States. Estimates are that three million U.S. citizens now have HCV. Prison populations in the United States have the highest concentration of HCV in the country, with about 17 percent of inmates estimated to have chronic HCV, while another 12 to 35 percent have the infection that leads to chronic HCV. Some researchers call HCV the silent epidemic, because often a person has no noticeable symptoms for up to 20 to 30 years after being infected; this means that most of those who have HCV do not know it.

A high percentage of Canadian inmates are infected with HCV as well. Studies done in the late 2000s indicated that almost a quarter of inmates have the disease. Many prisoners come to prison already infected, but prison conditions make it easy to spread diseases further—and HCV spreads more easily than HIV. HCV can lead to liver disease and liver cancer. Proper drug therapy, although expensive, can essentially cure the disease.

Some state prisons in the United States avoid testing and treating HCV patients because costs to treat the illness are so high. A 12-week course of medicines can run as much as $90,000. In 2000, the Texas Department of Corrections came up

Dr. John May, co-founder of Health through Walls at the AIDS TB-HIV Networking Zone discussing work to address TB-HIV among prisoners.

The Treatment of Prisoners and Prison Conditions   41

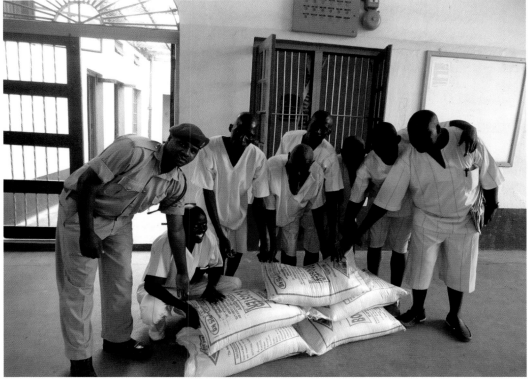

A prisons officer and some prisoners pose for a photo after receiving soya as part of the HIV and AIDS Training Programme in Uganda's Luzira Prison.

with a plan for testing, monitoring, and treating those with **chronic** infections, including HCV, and some other states say they give testing if requested. Prisoners in Minnesota and Massachusetts filed class action lawsuits to gain access to a simple HCV test. The cost: just $33 per person.

General Health Care

In an article on the LifeExtension website, "Health of Our Prisons," Jon VanZile described his interviews with dozens of former prison inmates concerning the quality of health care in U.S. prisons. Some rated the health care services as very good, but unfortunately, this was not the typical response. Due to the closed nature of prisons, researchers have difficulty getting an accurate picture of what medical care is like. If any checks and balances exist, they usually come from the inside—and sometimes no one checks. Meanwhile, the inmate population suffers from higher levels of illness such as cancer, heart disease, and infectious diseases than those found in the general public. VanZile says that according to inmate accounts, they are regularly required to wait for medical care, and when they get it, it is "woefully inadequate."

In the United States, incarceration health care varies from state to state. In a recent report, California state prisons' medical departments have admitted to being in shambles. They have stated that, despite spending two or three times as much as some other states on medical services, they have terrible medical facilities, and prisoners often die because of medical negligence and incompetent doctors. According to *San Francisco Chronicle* writer James Sterngold, some of the problems in the system include lack of nurses, doctors, and social workers to fill the job vacancies; prison salaries that are 30 to 40 percent lower than similar jobs in the public sector make these positions less attractive to employees. A report of San Quentin's facilities stated that inmates had no privacy during medical examinations, the rooms were dirty, and the records were unorganized. In 2006, California adopted HMO-style "managed care" procedures in a move toward improving care in its prisoner health system

Marvin Johnson, whose story is told in the book *Prison Nation: The Warehousing of America's Poor*, was arrested one morning for driving an acquaintance's car without permission. When arrested, he told three nurses and six sheriff's deputies that he was an insulin-dependent diabetic and needed his medicine. His girlfriend called the main jail headquarters to inform officials of his diabetic needs. When she offered to bring his medications, the officials told her they would take good care of him. Later, the nurse in charge accused Johnson of "faking" his condition, and in the end, the jail staff never gave Johnson his necessary shots, saying that he was vague about his medical history and that they could not confirm his prescription.

Less than three days after his arrest, he fell into a coma and died. Correctional Medical Services (or CMS, now known as Corizon) claims they did not get a report of Marvin's girlfriend calling the authorities. Annie Johnson, who helped to raise Johnson and his three siblings, sued the Shetland CMS for medical malpractice, negligence, and wrongful death. In 2013, a jury awarded her an $8.5 million settlement.

The company in charge of medical services at the jail where Marvin died was CMS—the largest health care provider to jails and prisons in the United States. As of 2015 Corizon (formerly CMS) served more than 345,000 inmates in 530 prisons and jails in 27 states. Unfortunately, Corizon has had many complaints against it for giving substandard medical care. It has a history of hiring doctors and other health care workers with records of lawsuits filed against them for malpractice and sexual assaults. In many states, the practice of hiring doctors who have had their licenses revoked is common because such incompetent medical workers turn to prisons as their last resort for employment. Many parties have filed lawsuits against CMS for wrongful deaths and lack of proper medical actions. In one rebuttal to a suit, a spokesperson stated that CMS was unfairly blamed for the problems of the jail. He claimed that inadequate

funding for jail services, an old facility, and extreme overcrowding were to blame in the case.

Under the Eighth Amendment of the U.S. Constitution, prison authorities are required to give inmates adequate medical care known as the "community standard" of health care. In other words, prisons are required to give the same level of care the outside community gives itself. Federal, state, and local prison systems, however, have deteriorated because of the indifference of the general population, a huge prison population explosion, and budget cuts. Because of these issues, although many dedicated and sincere medical professionals work in prisons, many facilities lack adequate medical care.

North American prisons have complicated and interwoven problems. Just as overcrowding intensifies prisons' medical failures, overcrowding also contributes to another prison issue: violence.

Hospitals and health care within the prison system are constantly in need of improvements.

Text-Dependent Questions

1. What kinds of problems are mentally ill prisoners more subject to in prison?
2. What two highly communicable diseases are more rampant in prisons than in the general population?
3. What corporation handles the medical care for more than 300,000 inmates?

Research Projects

1. Besides not being taken seriously and a lack of resources, what are some other roadblocks inmates face in seeking proper medical care?
2. Why are prisoners with demonstrated mental illnesses placed in prison instead of a mental health institution?

4 Violence

Words to Understand

Austere: Severely plain and simple.

Impending: About the happen.

Institutionalized atrocity: Became established as a custom or an accepted part of a larger structure.

Shanks: Makeshift knives made out of other objects.

John King was a common burglar when he went to prison. While at a Texas state prison, however, he was forced to interact with the race-based prison gangs. He coped by joining one—a white supremacist group that taught him violence and racial hatred. Upon his release, he and two other men killed an African American man, James Byrd Jr., by dragging him behind a truck. His case illustrates an all-too-common occurrence: prisoners incarcerated for nonviolent crimes often become violent people.

A former inmate in Pennsylvania also learned violence while serving time in juvenile detention. Daily fights were normal, so he learned how to be aggressive, give orders, and fight his way to the top. When released, he used robbery to support himself, and he ended up shooting and killing a man. He then served 18 years for homicide.

Testimonies of violence in prisons are numerous. Prisoners face **austere** and violent conditions. Guards must always be on the watch for their own safety. Male-on-male rape is common, and racial gangs dominate inmate life. In U.S. prisons, inmate attacks on prison staff have risen by 50 percent since the early 1990s.

In *The Oxford History of the Prison*, a prisoner writes of his daily routine: "A sense of **impending** danger is always with you; you must be careful to move around people rather than against them or through them, but with care and reasonable sense you can move safely enough." His life is not a constant experience of fights, threats, plots, and **shanks** (prison-made knives)—though he has

Guards outside California's famous San Quentin State Prison, which houses the founder of the violent Los Angeles street gang, the Crips. Gang members in prison tend to bring the violence of the streets with them.

to constantly watch those around him. For this prisoner and many like him, the biggest problem is monotony and boredom. Every day is the same; the idleness and boredom of it all wears him down. In conditions like this, violence may provide prisoners with drama and even entertainment.

Inmate-on-Guard Violence

Sometimes while guarding inmates, violence is inflicted on prison guards. In July 2015, guard Timothy Davison was routinely escorting a prisoner named Billy Joel Tracy from an activity room back to his cell at the Telford Unit, a maximum-security prison in Texas. During the transfer, Tracy grabbed an undisclosed item from Davison, and beat him to death with it. Davison had only been working at the prison for seven months; Tracy had been serving a life sentence since 1998 for aggravated assault and burglary, plus 45 years for a previous assault on a guard. Guards who have worked for many years in the system learn to "read" prisoners to avoid situations like this one. Prison staff usually know how to sense trouble before it happens and how to control cellblocks. Every day, guards hope to finish their shift and go home without any problems.

A maximum security cell block at Robben Island Prison.

Inmate-on-Inmate Violence

In March 30, 2012, an inmate at the Santa Rosa Correctional Institution in Florida named Ricky Martin was found dead in his cell. In addition to a bed sheet wrapped around his neck, Martin's skull had been smashed and he had cuts all over his body. His cries for help reportedly went unanswered. Martin's murderer was the only other person who had been in the cell: his cellmate Shawn Rogers, a violent offender who had repeatedly been reprimanded for attacking other inmates. Martin was a convicted burglar serving out the final months of a short sentence; he'd been transferred to Santa Rosa just 36 hours before Rogers killed him.

It is common for other inmates to kill an informant (a "snitch") in prison. Because of this, many violent incidents behind bars go unreported. An experienced corrections officer commented to *CBC News* that he was not surprised at the murder of an informant. The officer said that violence is on the rise in the Canadian prison system, and all penitentiaries are dangerous. Violence could break out at any time.

Gang Warfare

In the United States, many prisoners join a gang or a clique for protection. They must prove their eligibility first, but if they were in a gang on the outside or they are gang members from another prison, they are automatically eligible. Those who belong to gangs can be either a core member or an affiliate. Core members are the most active in gang activities; they rob other prisoners, control homosexual interactions, deal drugs, and fight with other gangs. The associates are not involved as closely with these activities, but they are ready if the gang needs a larger display of force, or to help in some operation such as smuggling drugs. Associates have the protection of the gang and can walk more freely in prison public places.

Prison officials try to cut down on gang violence by determining which prisoners are gang leaders and core members and putting them in maximum-security units. These prisoners may then stay there for many years. In Texas, for example, gang leaders stay in these "super-max" units until they have served their sentence. This practice has not stopped gang activity, however. Gang attacks and murders of other inmates and guards continue in the general prison population.

The majority of prisoners, especially those serving sentences for the first time, stay away from other prisoners and large gatherings of inmates. They stay with a few friends whom they may have met on their cellblocks, on the outside, in other prisons, or at their assigned prison work. Some choose to stay in their cell most of the time. Despite these practices, the number of gang members and associates rose in many prison systems in the last few years, most notably in the Luzerne County Correctional Facility in northeastern Pennsylvania. At this and other institutions, overcrowding makes it difficult for staff to separate inmates with different gang affiliations.

It's not easy to determine which violent incidents gangs have caused. Each facility has a staff person designated to work with the area police and the Royal Canadian Mounted Police to identify and control gang members. According to a report by Inmate Services and Conditions of Custody, in Saskatchewan Correctional Centres, however, officials take several measures to cut down on possible gang violence. If an inmate is a known gang member, for example, he will not be able to get any work education training placement that may give status to gang membership. He cannot wear any gang-related items or keep property that endorses gang membership. Officials conduct frequent room and property checks to make sure inmates obtained their personal items through appropriate means, and officials also censor mail and telephone correspondence.

Gangs in Prison

Documentary on gang violence in U.S. prisons.

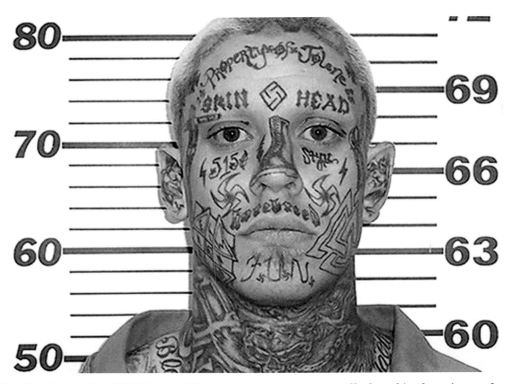

The Nazi Lowriders (NLR) is a white supremacist gang generally found in the prisons of southern California.

Many gang members have tattoos. This Dead Man Incorporated gang member proudly shows his tattoos.

Prison Rape

Prison rape is an unpleasant subject that many in society choose to ignore. According to Lovisa Stannow, executive director of Just Detention International (JDI), prison rape is an **institutionalized atrocity** that goes against a person's most basic human rights, causes the spread of disease, and creates a violent cycle both inside and outside prison walls.

A recent study done on four Midwestern state prisons reported that one in five male prisoners reported a forced or pressured sexual experience while in prison. According to Just Detention, more than 200,000 inmates (mostly male) are raped in the United States every year. Rates for female rape differ greatly among facilities, and the rapists are usually male staff workers. According to a 2014 Human Rights Watch report, 15 percent of female inmates reported a pressured or forced sexual incident. Of those, a male perpetrator—in other words, a male staffer—was reported to be responsible 98 percent of the time.

Studies show that juveniles placed in adult prisons are five times more likely to be victims of sexual assault than youth in juvenile detentions. Many states are sentencing more and more youth offenders as adults, which results in growing amounts of abuse. According to JDI the suicide rate is 7.7 times higher for young people in adult institutions than in youth detention centers.

Anyone can become a victim, but certain characteristics make some more vulnerable than others. Men incarcerated for the first time and nonviolent offenders are prime targets. Many of these have no gang affiliations to protect them and are not able to protect themselves. Prisoners often attack smaller, younger men who are somewhat feminine. Gay men are often targets. For women, specific characteristics do not play such a large part in deciding victims of abuse, but younger, first-time offenders and women who are mentally disabled are more likely targets.

Many times, male victims of rape become targets for more attacks. They accept sexual slavery to a powerful inmate in order to survive. Other prisoners treat them like property or force them into prostitution. For some, barbaric assaults by gangs or individuals have left them bleeding, beaten, and sometimes dead.

The "Shame, Depression, and Terror" of Prison Rape

The horrors experienced by many young inmates, particularly those who are convicted of nonviolent offenses, border on the unimaginable. Prison rape not only threatens the lives of those who fall prey to their aggressors, but it is potentially devastating to the human spirit. Shame, depression, and a shattering loss of self-esteem accompany the perpetual terror the victim thereafter must endure.

—U.S. SUPREME COURT JUSTICE HARRY A. BLACKMUN, *FARMER V. BRENNAN*

Sexual Assaults and Disease

Sexual assaults can be a death sentence to the victim if the rapist is infected with HIV or HCV. Women can end up pregnant and be denied proper medical services. Some of the psychological effects are shock, insomnia, disbelief, anger, guilt, withdrawal, humiliation, and shame. Many prisoners go through long-term effects, such as ongoing fear, flashbacks, substance abuse, posttraumatic stress disorder, depression, anxiety, and suicide. Male survivors sometimes suppress their extreme anger over the incident until release from prison, when they become involved in antisocial and violent behavior in the community. Some become rapists themselves, trying to gain back a feeling of masculinity.

Prison rape is also very costly to the public. Expenses may involve lawsuits, reincarceration, recidivism, and higher amounts of substance abuse, mental health services, and medical care for sexually transmitted diseases.

CBC News asked the question, "Do you think Canada's prisons are too soft?" Many wrote letters answering, yes. One young woman wrote the following:

> *If you think that Canada's prisons are too soft…find a room that is about eight by six feet, move in your bed, some shelves, a small writing table, a TV, some books, a coffee maker, and with some luck, a chair. Put a toilet in the extra space left over, and hope that maybe you will have a window. Plan to stay there for at least two years. In most prisons, you get to come out of your room for meals and a half hour each day for yard or library time.*
>
> *In the morning you get up to make sure someone did not rape you or stab you in your sleep. Someone opens your door for you—you can't just go and come as you please. As you are walking around, always be on your guard. Make sure to be careful whom you look at and how, it could get you killed. Don't express yourself too much and you might stay alive.*

Prison overcrowding makes it difficult to provide simple rape prevention techniques, such as grouping cellmates together according to risk. Rapes usually occur when no one is around to see or hear the event. Sometimes they happen at night in poorly lit places; inmates report that often their screams for help are unanswered. When prisoners report victimization by a rapist, the common procedure is to put the victim in administrative segregation, similar to solitary confinement. This is hard for most prisoners to endure, and this practice discourages them from reporting the crime.

The judicial system also appears to lack any concern about prison rape: many prosecutors are not interested in taking cases between inmates. They usually leave internal prison matters to prison authorities, who in turn do not often push for trials for inmate-on-inmate abuses. Authorities rarely punish rapists, whether they are prisoners or staff members. Some victims have reported that prison workers have retaliated when the inmate filed a complaint against them. Prisons workers have used rape as a tool to punish some inmates, putting them in the same cell as known rapists and ignoring their pleas for help.

Prison Riots

Prison riots usually happen in protest against prison conditions and when relations between inmates and prison officials break down. From 1971 to 1992, at least 14 major prison riots took place in the United States. The two worst were at Attica, a New York State prison, in 1971, and at New Mexico State Penitentiary in 1980. In the Attica riot, state officers killed 32 unarmed prisoners and 11 prison employees. Four of the prison workers and all the inmates died of gunfire inflicted by police regaining control. Prison inmates killed 33 prisoners in the New Mexico riot. Many of the murdered prisoners had been in protective custody, and fellow prisoners thought they were informers.

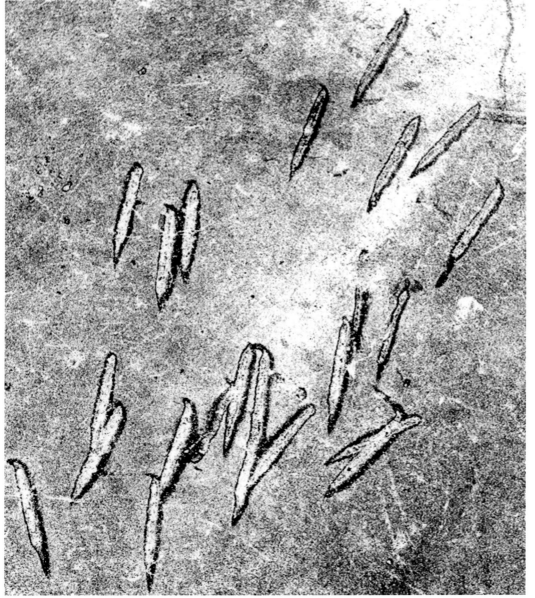

Axe marks pit the floor where a prisoner was tortured during the New Mexico State Penitentiary riot.

Attica Correctional Facility in New York keeps a memorial to the terrible riot in 1971.

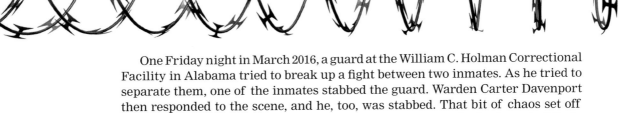

One Friday night in March 2016, a guard at the William C. Holman Correctional Facility in Alabama tried to break up a fight between two inmates. As he tried to separate them, one of the inmates stabbed the guard. Warden Carter Davenport then responded to the scene, and he, too, was stabbed. That bit of chaos set off unrest, which included more than 100 prisoners rioting, who broke out of their housing unit and started a fire. With the aid of a contraband cell phone, inmates published photos and videos of the riots to social media.

Kingston Penitentiary in Canada was the site of one of Canada's largest riots. In 1971, inmates took over the facilities for four days, and rioters released 641 prisoners from their cellblocks. In the end, two inmates died, and the interior of the cellblock was destroyed. Prisonjustice.ca states that the riot was in reaction to the upcoming transfer of inmates and guards to Millhaven, the new, maximum-security prison. Rumors said this new facility had cells bugged so that guards could hear every word a prisoner said.

After the riot, Canadian officials established the Commission of Inquiry to start looking into the Kingston riot as well as several other disturbances at other penal institutions in the Canadian system. The commission found the need for a better way to address inmate complaints, and so the Office of the Correctional Investigator was formed to work on behalf of inmates.

Addressing the Underlying Anger

Despite this step, inmates rioted at Kent Prison in British Columbia in 2003. The reason cited was the inmates' anger over recent changes at the institution: authorities had made new rules banning group meetings of prisoners, enforcing the wearing of prison uniforms, and making all inmates eat inside their cells. One prisoner died in the struggle.

In Manitoba, Canada, the correction facilities use a system that attempts to measure the volatility of the environment. Staff members fill out a checklist reporting any increases in telephone calls, hand signals, canteen purchases, requests for protection, and visitor cancellations, along with any decreases in communications, eye contact, and prisoner participation in programs. Changes in these activities may indicate a violent event is brewing.

Riots seem to happen more often in the larger, overcrowded prisons where there is idleness and racial tension. Gangs are often the cause of riots. Sometimes a harsh environment makes the prison like a bomb "waiting to explode." All too often, abuse plays a major role in the explosion.

Text-Dependent Questions

1. What's a shank?
2. Why might prisoners join a gang if they were not gang-affiliated before prison?
3. Who are the main culprits in sexual assaults on female inmates? What about in assaults on male inmates?

Research Projects

1. Besides the Prison Rape Elimination Act, what are some other ways that the government has tried to decrease sexual assaults in prison?
2. What are some ways that prisons have tried to address the issue of prison rape?

Excessive Force

Words to Understand

Caustic: Corrosive.

Indicted: Formally charged someone with a crime.

Inquest: A formal legal investigation.

In Texas, a 31-year-old man diagnosed with schizophrenia had a psychotic episode on the night of July 6, 1999. Delusional and believing that a relative was chasing and trying to murder him, he ran to the police for safety. Unfortunately, this was not his safest option, and by the end of the night, he was dead.

According to *Prison Nation: The Warehousing of America's Poor*, the police sprayed the delusional man with pepper spray and then put him in a restraining chair. Police did not allow him to wash the spray out of his eyes or face, which is a violation of department procedures. His mother's lawyer stated, "He was not decontaminated, and he was left alone in a room. Within 20 minutes he was dead."

Although many detention officers, police, and prison staff may be dedicated to the welfare of inmates, some are all too prone to abusive behavior. Amnesty International has been telling the U.S. Congress for many years that cruelty does not just happen in other countries; it is happening in U.S. prisons today. National awareness is growing as stories of prison brutality eventually make their way to public knowledge.

Misuse of Restraints

The electric chair is not the only dreaded chair in penitentiaries and jails. Some prison employees have called the other chair the "we care chair," the "be sweet chair," the "strap-o-lounger," and the "barca-lounger." Some inmates and their lawyers call it "slave chair," "torture chair," and "devil's chair." It is a restraining chair intended for the most violent prisoners. Testimonies of prisoners and lawyers, as well as reviews of jail videotapes, court cases, and scattered news stories,

An electric taser, or stun gun, is one method of controlling inmates that has been involved in excessive force.

A contemporary prison cell in Germany.

report that the restraint chair is being used improperly and sometimes in a sadistic manner.

In the 1999 Texas case, the manufacturers of the police department's chair, KLK, Inc., of Phoenix, called their product a "Violent Person Restraint Chair." They are proud to say that it had been used by a very large jail system for four years, with a 90 percent reduction of injuries compared to the previous four years. KLK sells these chairs mainly to prisons and hospitals, and it insists that the chair is not responsible for anyone's death: the issue is how the chair is used. Meanwhile, however, an attorney in Atlanta claims that the mere presence of any restraint chair is asking for abuse.

Prison Nation says authorities have used restraint chairs for children who were demonstrating nonviolent but annoying behavior. Officials have also used these chairs on adult detainees and inmates for up to eight days at a time. Inmates have been tortured while pepper sprayed and hooded, forced to testify, interrogated, threatened, or beaten. Some prisoners

A Pro-Straint® Restraint Chair is one of the most feared methods of restraint used in prison

have been strapped in a restraint chair in the nude. In the United States, at least 11 people have died after being strapped into these chairs—and yet the chair has become popular in U.S. jails, federal and state prisons, juvenile detention centers, the U.S. Citizenship and Immigration Services, state mental hospitals, and the U.S. Marshals Service.

In late 1996, a woman died at the Connecticut Valley Hospital after authorities held her for 33 hours in a restraint chair in a local jail. When they released her, blood clots that had formed in her legs traveled to her lungs, killing her. A Maricopa County, AZ, man died in June 1996 after prison guards gagged him, pushed him into a restraint chair, forced his head to his chest, and shocked him with a stun gun. The county coroner said his death was an accident, but the courts later ruled that the man's death was a direct result of his time spent in the restraint chair. In 2012, authorities at Iowa's Jasper County Jail placed Richard Watson in a restraint chair and locked him in a cell. He wasn't given food, water, or access to his high blood pressure medication (which he informed staff he needed). After 20 hours, staff checked in on Watson and found him dead.

The Sacramento, CA, sheriff's department settled a lawsuit claiming that deputies were torturing people with a restraint chair. According to former inmates, the guards strapped prisoners in the chair and told them they would electrocute them. A 106-pound woman claimed to have been strapped in the chair for eight and a half hours with the restraining straps so tight they cut off circulation in her legs and arms, and sliced the skin from her back and shoulders. She alleges that prison workers mocked and taunted her while they denied her water or use of the bathroom.

Canada, meanwhile, has only six restraint chairs. Officials use the chair at times for suicidal inmates or those high on drugs. John Schofield, Newfoundland's superintendent of prisons, says prison workers use the chairs solely for the protection of the prisoner or the other prisoners—but according to a prisoner rights advocate with the John Howard Society, former inmates say differently. They say guards use it as a form of punishment. Shortly after an inmate took a guard hostage at the Nova Institution for Women in Nova Scotia, staff weren't taking any chances with 19-year-old Ashley Smith. In August 2007, Smith, who was on suicide watch, banged her head on the floor of her cell and as punishment she was placed in a restraint chair for eight hours. Video of Smith in the chair was used as evidence at an **inquest** investigating if the use of excessive force led to Smith's prison suicide two months after the incident. (Smith's family and the Correctional Service of Canada reached an out-of-court settlement.)

In the United States, there are efforts to ban or restrict the use of the restraint chair. In 1999, a Knox County, TN, judge ruled the confession of a robbery suspect was involuntary and illegal because authorities had held him for five hours in a restraint chair. Amnesty International has called for a review of the use of restraint chairs in jails and prisons based on evidence of its misuse. A criminal court judge stated that, although the restraint chair might be useful, it could easily cross the line into being a coercive force.

A prisoner subjected to abuse by U.S. forces at the Abu Ghriab prison in Iraq.

Chemical Sprays and Electric Shocks

Pictures of torture at Abu Ghraib, a prison in Baghdad, Iraq, shocked the world in 2004. Deborah Davies, a British reporter for the BBC, channel 4, conducted a four-month investigation on prisons in the United States to see if there was an explanation for Americans' actions in Iraq. She obtained videos of prisoners experiencing what she calls "wholesale torture" inside U.S. prisons. She did not base her findings on rumors or hearsay but on solid evidence from videos from all across the United States. In many states, when guards need to exert force, they are required to videotape the event to prove they did not use excessive force—but many tapes prove the opposite.

Multiple lawyers who spoke to Deborah Davies agreed that abuse in U.S. prisons happens all the time. One lawyer pointed as proof to mountains of files stacked on his desk and floor, files filled with stories of alarming treatment inside U.S. prisons. Davies got her videotapes from lawyers who got them from reluctant state prisons for use during drawn-out lawsuits.

Pepper spray and electric taser guns are two methods of "controlling" prisoners. An Amnesty International report details the **caustic** effects of pepper spray: The mucous membranes of the eyes, nose, and mouth become inflamed, causing the eyes to close. The victim experiences shortness of breath, gagging, coughing, and a terrible burning sensation on the skin and inside the mouth and nose. The effects are extremely unpleasant.

According to a report by *The Nation*, the warden at West Virginia's maximum security Mount Olive Correctional Complex has declared "martial law" on his prisoners and will use any and all methods of crowd control at his disposal. Among his most favorite techniques is authorizing guards to use grenade-launchers to dispense grenades outfitted with military-grade tear gas.

Many times guards use pepper spray for trivial reasons. Deborah Davies found that some of the reasons for spraying inmates include banging on their doors and refusing medications. Prisoners report telltale signs that guards are about to spray them: prison workers place cardboard under their door to make sure the room is airtight, while they cut off ventilation fans. One lawyer explained that guards usually use fire-extinguisher-size canisters full of pepper spray. He has seen prisoners with second-degree burns from the pepper spray all over their bodies. Some have been sprayed and "left to cook in the burning fog of chemicals." One lawyer showed Davies pictures of his client with a large burned patch on his hip. Another photo showed an inmate with a terrible rash across his neck, back, and arms.

In January 2005, two prisoners died in Alabama. One was pepper sprayed and one was tasered. A tape from Florida also shows a prisoner tasered for refusing orders. As he lies on an examining table, the guards instruct him to climb down into a wheelchair. He yells, "I can't, I can't!" and, "It hurts!" A guard then jabs him on both hips with a taser. As the electricity hits him, the man jerks and screams but he still will not get into the chair. The guards grab him and force him into the chair. When they try to bend his legs to fit the footrest, he shrieks in pain. The video ends showing the guards trying to make the prisoner walk with a walker. He falls on the floor crying in pain, and they taser him again. He finally lays there moaning because he has run out of energy and breath to cry. The man's lawyer told Davies that his client had a very limited mental capacity, plus he had a back problem that caused him to have terrible pain when he walked or bent his legs.

The taser isn't the only voltage-based form of punishment. Despite calls for bans from several human rights groups, in 2014, the California Supreme Court upheld the right for prisons to use a device called the Remote Electronically Activated Control Technology, or "stun belt." It's a four-inch-wide band the prisoner wears under his clothes that can deliver an eight-second shock of 50,000 volts of electricity. It causes severe muscle pain and can incapacitate an inmate for as long as 45 minutes.

Inside a Maximum-Security Prison

See what it's like to live in a maximum-security prison.

The U.S. armed forces undergo pepper spray demonstrations. Each must experience being sprayed in the face with pepper spray during training.

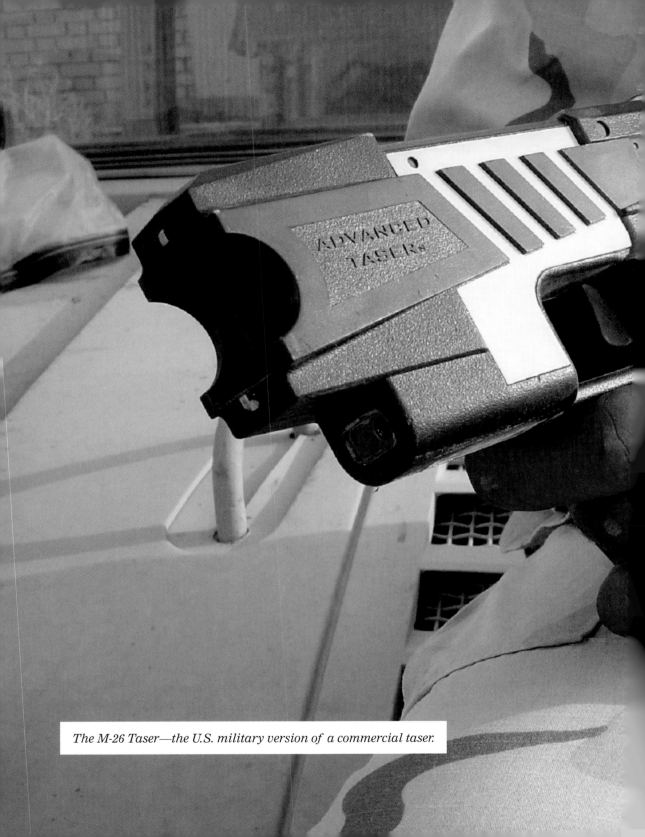

The M-26 Taser—the U.S. military version of a commercial taser.

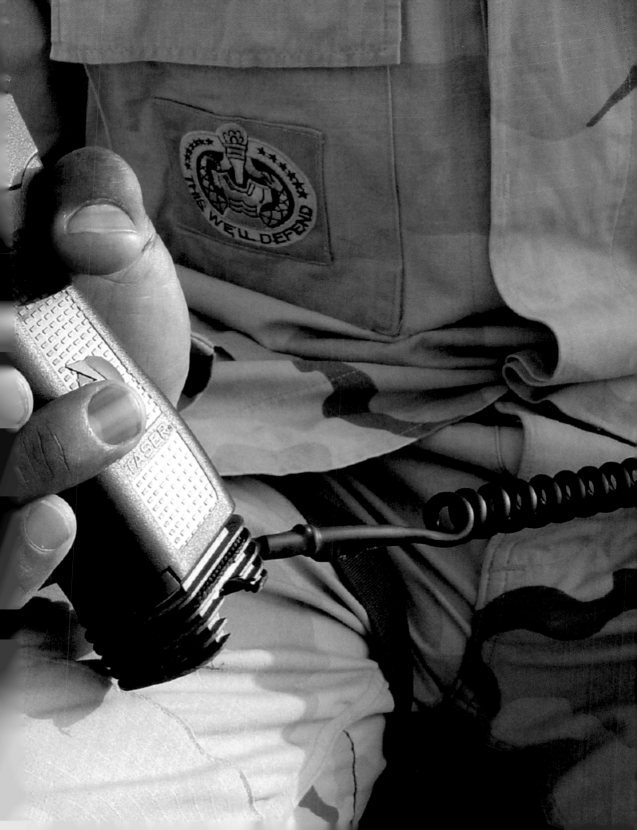

Guard Abuse of Inmates

Officials regarded it as one of the foremost high-tech prisons in the United States when it was first built in 1993. The Federal Correctional Complex in Florence, Colorado, had lower security facilities, a maximum-security unit, and an administrative maximum-security facility. It also had brutal guards who called themselves the Cowboys. Due to media exposure, complaints from other prison staff, and many lawsuits filed by inmates, in 1999, the public got a view of how the guards at Florence abused prisoners.

The Worst of the Worst

Scholars argue whether corruption and cruelty among guards is due to the conditions they see every day in their workplace or is something that springs from their own personalities. Victor Hassine, author of *Life Without Parole*, has seen firsthand that personalities change in prison. He believes that "even the gentlest person in the world will become violent after spending five years in a prison like Graterford. . . . What goes for prisoners also goes for prison staff." Hassine thinks it is logical that if understaffed and overcrowded prisons teach criminality, rage, and violence to inmates, they will also affect the staff that spend much of their waking hours in the same environment.

Prison Nation tells how guards at Florence bashed the heads of inmates into walls, kicked them, and mixed feces and urine into their food. Once, two guards threw a burning piece of paper into a cell to justify spraying the men inside with a fire extinguisher. Many prisoners suffered at the hands of these men.

The Cowboys formed in 1995 as a secret gang of disgruntled guards. They believed that prisoners assigned to the Special Housing Unit (SHU) for attacking staff were punished too lightly—so they decided to kick, hit, and torture cuffed and chained prisoners, and then falsely document that the prisoners provoked the violence. The Cowboys threatened physical harm to officers who stood up to them in defense of inmates. A former Florence guard said he and others told management about the abuse many times, but management did nothing to stop it.

On November 2, 2000, a court **indicted** seven members of the Cowboys, charging them with 52 acts of misconduct against 20 specific prisoners from 1995 to 1997. The attorney representing the guards claimed that the prisoners trumped up false charges. The president of the local union stood up for the accused guards, saying they had been good guards. The former union leaders who blew the whistle on the Cowboys to the Bureau of Prisons were not elected the following term. The candidate who won denied that anything wrong happened. He had the union set up a fund for the families of accused guards while the case was pending. If not for the undaunted reports of a local writer and the guards who testified against their cohorts, the abuse at Florence might have continued.

Of course not all prison guards are abusive. A great many prison workers fulfill the duties of their difficult work with professionalism, and some go beyond that, showing genuine care for inmates. Author Victor Hassine was surprised at how well guards and inmates generally got along at his Pennsylvania prison. He found no open hostility between the two groups; instead, many officials and prisoners went out of their way to make good relationships. If good relationships were established, both inmates and guards knew they would benefit. Inmates hoped for special benefits, such as increased shower time or an extra phone call, and guards hoped for easy-to-handle prisoners and their own personal safety.

Female Inmates

Some North Americans feel that prison facilities discriminate against women. Women are a small group of prisoners who do not usually need maximum-security facilities, yet officials place most of them in high-security facilities anyway. Women do not have the same accessibility to programs, halfway houses, family contact, or education. They need specialized medical care, such as gyne-cological, prenatal, and postnatal care. Women also need their own services for overcoming drug and alcohol abuse, and they need counseling provided by women to help with abuse issues. Because women are more often responsible for the care of both parents in their elderly years and young children, incarcerated women need parenting services.

In 2000, the Prison for Women closed in Kingston, ON, and the government shipped women to isolated areas of men's prisons. Since then, the rates of women prisoners' suicide attempts and self-destruction have gone up. "Women try to find a way out of these inhumane conditions, even through death," one female prisoner shared on Prisonjustice.ca.

In Canada, according to some concerned citizens, certain women are especially at risk in prisons. Kim Pate, the executive director of the Canadian Association of Elizabeth Fry Societies, believes that prisons especially discriminate against Aboriginal women and women with disabilities. The Disabled Women's Network Canada believes that authorities are discriminating against federally sentenced females with mental and developmental disabilities. Officials see mental disabil-ity as a danger. If a woman is suicidal or has cognitive or mental disabilities, authorities might put her in isolation, without clothes, in a barren cell. The prison has become a substitute for community-based mental health services. In 2003, the Prisoner's Justice Day Committee, along with women's groups and prisoner's rights groups across Canada, asked the Correctional Service of Can-ada as well as the government of Canada to end the discriminating treatment of women in prison and to close the new maximum-security prisons for women.

Special Abuse Issues Faced by Female Inmates

Female inmates in the United States sometimes go through the awful experi-ence of being pregnant while in prison. Two women in a Michigan facility told Amnesty International that officials took them to the hospital in a belly chain and handcuffs. One of the women had her legs shackled together. Officials re-moved her restraints just before the birth of her child only at the insistence of the doctor, but the guard had to get permission from the prison first. Guards

Demolition of the wall of the former Prison for Women, Kingston, ON, Canada. Opened in 1934, the prison was closed in 2000. The building has been purchased by Queen's University.

A correctional officer monitors female inmates.

handcuffed the other woman to the bed until the baby was just about to be born and again handcuffed both women to their beds immediately after they gave birth.

The female inmates confided in Amnesty International that, in spite of an investigation by the U.S. Justice Department into sexual abuse of female inmates in Michigan and the consequent legal action that took place, guards were still sexually abusing female inmates. The inmates said that guards watched women in the showers or when dressing, sexually assaulted them, and touched them inappropriately during pat searches. They also told of inadequate medical attention. Amnesty International spoke with two female guards who confirmed the stories that sexual abuse is a pattern in female incarceration units. If the female inmates complained, they were threatened or punished. One guard reported that she was harassed after she complained about the sexual behavior of the guards, and, eventually, she was beaten and slashed. Amnesty International has heard the same sort of reports from inmates in some other states as well.

Text-Dependent Questions

1. Describe a restraint chair.
2. How does pepper spray affect a person?
3. List three types of excessive force.

Research Projects

1. What are some forms of punishment and prisoner control that have been outlawed in certain states or nationally?
2. Find more examples of prisoner abuse by guards that was noticed, stopped, and prosecuted.

Series Glossary

Abolition: The act of officially ending a law or practice.

Acquitted: Declared not guilty by a court or judge.

Adjudicated: Made a legal decision.

Advocacy: Active support for a cause or position.

Allegations: Statements saying someone has done something wrong or illegal.

Arbitrary: Based on whim or chance instead of logic.

Arson: The willful and malicious burning of property.

Asylum: Protection given by a government to someone who has left another country to escape being harmed.

At-risk: In danger of being harmed or damaged; in danger of failing or committing a crime.

Chronic: Something that is long term or recurs frequently.

Civil rights: Basic rights that all citizens of a society are supposed to have.

Coerce: Force someone to do something he or she does not want to do.

Community service: Unpaid work performed for the benefit of the local community that an offender is required to do instead of going to prison.

Constitutional freedoms: Rights to which every United states citizen is entitled as guaranteed by the Constitution. these include the right to free speech, to a free press, to practice one's religion, and to assemble peaceably.

Corporal punishment: Punishment that involves inflicting physical pain.

Court-martialed: Tried and convicted in a military court.

Defendant: In a criminal trial, the person accused of a crime.

Disposition: Settlement of a legal matter.

Detainees: People being detained, or kept in prison.

Disposition: Settlement of a legal matter.

Dissidents: Those who publicly disagree with an established political or religious system or organization.

Electronic monitoring: Electronic or telecommunications system, such as an ankle bracelet transmitter, used to track and supervise the location of an individual.

Exile: A punishment that forces a person to leave his or her country; also known as banishment.

Exonerated: Cleared of criminal charges or declared not guilty.

Extenuating circumstances: Reasons that excuse or justify someone's actions.

Extortion: The crime of obtaining something from someone using illegal methods of persuasion.

Extrajudicial: Outside normal legal proceedings.

Felonies: Serious crimes for which the punishment is usually imprisonment for more than a year.

Fraud: The crime of obtaining money or other benefit by the use of deliberate deception.

Grievance: A written complaint, delivered to authorities for resolution.

Halfway house: A residence for individuals after release from institutionalization (for a mental disorder, drug addiction, or criminal activity) that is designed to facilitate their readjustment to private life.

Hearing: Formal discussion of an inmates' case before a judge.

Humane: Having or displaying compassion.

Hunger strike: A refusal to eat, usually carried out by a prisoner as a form of protest.

Indicted: Formally charged someone with a crime.

Industrialized: Adapted to industrial methods of production and manufacturing.

Inherent: Innate or characteristic of something, and therefore unable to be considered separately.

Inhumane: Without compassion; cruel.

Inquest: A formal legal investigation.

Jurisdiction: A territory over which a government or agency has legal authority.

Larceny: The unlawful taking of personal property from another.

Lynching: Seizing someone believed to have committed a crime and putting him or her to death immediately and without trial, often by hanging.

Mandate: An order handed down by a governmental authority.

Misdemeanors: Minor crimes considered less serious than felonies.

Objective: Unbiased by personal feelings or interpretations.

Organized crime: Criminal activities that are widespread and centrally controlled like a business.

Parole: The early release of a prisoner with specified requirements, such as the need to report to authorities for a specified period.

Penology: The study of the treatment of criminals and incarceration.

Peremptory: Not open to debate or discussion.

Plea bargains: The negotiations of agreements between prosecutors and defendants whereby defendants are permitted to plead guilty to reduced charges.

Precedent: An action or decision that can be used as an example for a later decision or to justify a similar action.

Probation: A period where an offender is released from prison but placed under supervision.

Protocols: Detailed rules and plans.

Psychotherapy: The treatment of mental illness through analysis or talk therapy.

Public-order crimes: Victimless crimes, such as prostitution.

Punitive: Inflicting or intended as punishment.

Quarantine: To separate to prevent contact.

Radical: Extreme.

Recidivism: The repeating of or returning to criminal behavior. The recidivism rate is the percentage of released prisoners who go on to commit new crimes.

Rehabilitation: To help someone return to good standing in the community.

Retribution: Punishment.

Repent: To express regret and seek forgiveness for past deeds, such as crimes.

Restitution: The act of making good or giving an equivalent for some injury.

Self-incrimination: The act of offering evidence or statements that would strongly suggest one's own guilt.

Shanks: Makeshift knives made out of other objects.

Sociopaths: People whose behavior is antisocial and who lack a conscience.

Status offender: A young person charged with an offense, such as running away from home or skipping school repeatedly, that would not be considered a crime if committed by an adult.

Suspended sentences: Punishments that are not carried out so long as the person meets certain conditions.

Therapeutic: Helpful toward solving or curing a physical problem or illness.

Tribunal: A court or forum of justice.

Truancy: Being absent from school without an excuse.

Vagrancy: A lifestyle characterized by wandering with no permanent place to live.

Work-release program: A program that allows trusted offenders to work outside the correctional facility.

Workhouses: Publicly supported buildings where usually very poor people worked in exchange for housing and food.

Further Resources

Websites

Amnesty International: amnesty.org

Bureau of Justice Statistics: http://www.bjs.gov/

The Education and Employment Ministry: Teem.org

Human Rights Watch: hrw.org

Just Detention International: http://justdetention.org/

Prisons in America: www.pbs.org/now/society/prisons3.html

Further Reading

Bartollas, Clemens, and Katherine Stuart van Wormer. *Women and the Criminal Justice System*. Needham Heights, MA: Allyn & Bacon, 2000.

Espejo, Roman, ed. *America's Prisons: Opposing Viewpoints*. San Diego, CA: Greenhaven Press, 2002.

Hassine, Victor. *Life Without Parole: Living in Prison Today*. Los Angeles, CA: Roxbury Publishing Company, 2000.

Herivel, Tara, and Paul Wright, eds. *Prison Nation: The Warehousing of America's Poor*. New York: Routledge, 2003.

Laci, Miklos. *Prisons and Jails: A Deterrent to Crime?* Farmington Hills, MI: Gale, 2004.

Lerner, Jimmy. *You Got Nothing Coming: Notes from a Prison Fish*. New York: Broadway Books, 2002.

Rabiger, Joanna. *Daily Prison Life*. Broomall, PA: Mason Crest Publishers, 2003.

Richards, Stephen C., and Jeffrey Ian Ross. *Behind Bars: Surviving Prison*. Indianapolis, IN: Alpha Books, 2002.

Index

Abu Ghraib prison 62

abuse 10, 14, 19, 23–25, 40, 52–53, 56, 60, 62, 68–69, 74

alternative sentencing 30–31

American Civil Liberties Union 37

Amnesty International 59, 61–62, 69, 74

armed robbery 22

bikers 14

boot camp 30

boredom 48

Bush, George W. 35

Canadian Association of Elizabeth Fry Societies (CAEFS) 35, 69

Canadian Criminal Justice Association (CCJA) 25

Canadian National Committee for Police/ Mental Health Liaison (CNCPMHL) 35

community service 30

conditional sentence 30

Cowboys, the 68

crime prevention 25

deadly weapons 14

discrimination 23–24

disease 19, 33, 37, 40, 42, 51–53, 74

electric chair 59

electric taser gun 62

excessive force 24, 59, 61–62

Federal Bureau of Prisons (FBOP) 12, 37

gangs 9–10, 14, 47, 49–52, 56, 68

hepatitis C (HCV) 40, 42, 52

HIV/AIDS 9, 36–37, 40–42, 52

Human Rights Watch 30, 34, 51

illegal drugs 24

informant 49

isolation 9–10, 69

maximum security 48–49, 56, 63, 68–69

mentally ill 24, 33–35

murder 12, 15, 18, 24–25, 49, 53, 59

organized crime 14

overcrowding 10, 19, 21–22, 24–25, 29–31, 44, 49, 53, 74

parole board 12, 23

pepper spray 59–60, 62–63, 65

posttraumatic stress disorder 52

protective custody 53

psychological therapy 19

race 13, 21, 47

rape 9–10, 13, 15, 24, 47, 51–53

reform 12, 19, 23

rehabilitation 18–19, 23, 74

restraining chair 59

riot 14, 25, 53–56

Royal Canadian Mounted Police 50

solitary confinement 15, 34–35, 53

suicide 34, 52, 61, 69

torture 15, 54, 59–60, 62, 68

understaffing 10, 22, 68

violence 9–10, 14, 19, 24–25, 34, 44, 47–50, 68, 74

vocational training 19

white supremacist 47, 50

About the Author

Roger Smith holds a degree in English education and formerly taught in the Los Angeles public schools. Smith did volunteer work with youthful inmates at a juvenile detention facility in Los Angeles. He currently lives in Arizona.

About the Series Consultant

Dr. Larry E. Sullivan is associate dean and chief librarian at the John Jay College of Criminal Justice and Professor of Criminal Justice in the doctoral program at the Graduate School and University Center of the City University of New York. He first became involved in the criminal justice system when he worked at the Maryland Penitentiary in Baltimore in the late 1970s. That experience prompted him to write the book *The Prison Reform Movement: Forlorn Hope* (1990; revised edition 2002). His most recent publication is the three-volume *Encyclopedia of Law Enforcement* (2005). He has served on a number of editorial boards, including the *Encyclopedia of Crime and Punishment*, and *Handbook of Transnational Crime and Justice*. At John Jay College, in addition to directing the largest and best criminal justice library in the world, he teaches graduate and doctoral level courses in criminology and corrections. John Jay is the only liberal arts college with a criminal justice focus in the United States. Internationally recognized as a leader in criminal justice education and research, John Jay is also a major training facility for local, state, and federal law enforcement personnel.

Picture Credits